The Eulogi

A Vision

William Hayley

Alpha Editions

This edition published in 2021

ISBN : 9789355114105

Design and Setting By
Alpha Editions
www.alphaedis.com
Email - info@alphaedis.com

THE EULOGIES OF HOWARD

It was my chance to be conversing with a Friend of the benevolent and indefatigable HOWARD, when our country was first afflicted with the public intelligence of his death. After our first expression of surprize and sorrow, we naturally fell into serious and affectionate reflections on the gentle character and sublime pursuits of the deceased. On these articles we had no difference of opinion; but in the course of our conversation a point arose, on which our sentiments were directly opposite, though we were equally sincere and ardent in our regret and veneration for the departed Worthy, to whom it related. I happened to speak of the public honours that, I hoped, a grateful, a generous, a magnificent Nation would render to his memory. My companion immediately exclaimed, "that every ostentatious memorial, to commemorate the virtues of his friend, would be inconsistent with the meekness and simplicity of the man; that all, who had the happiness of knowing HOWARD, must recollect with what genuine modesty he had ever retired from the enthusiastic admiration of those, who had hoped to gratify his ambition by undeserved applause; that he had really sought no reward but in the approbation of his conscience and his GOD; that the British Nation, however eminent for genius and munificence, could not devise any posthumous honours, or raise any monument, truly worthy of HOWARD, except in adopting and accomplishing those benevolent projects which his philanthropy and experience had recommended to public attention for the benefit of mankind."

I readily admitted the singular and unquestionable modesty of the deceased.—I allowed that the noblest tribute of respect, which the world could render to so pure a spirit, would be to realize his ideas; but I contended, that other honours are still due to his name; that it is the duty and the interest of mankind to commemorate his character with the fondest veneration. I reminded my companion, that although we were sincerely convinced that no human mind, engaged in great designs, could be more truly modest than that of HOWARD; yet we had particular reason to recollect, that he was not insensible to praise. He had once imparted to us his feelings on that subject with a frank and tender simplicity, highly graceful in an upright and magnanimous being, conscious of no sentiment that he could wish to conceal. Indeed, a sincere and ardent passion for virtue could hardly subsist with a disdain of true glory, which is nothing more than the proper testimony of intelligent and honed admiration to the existence of merit: nor is it reasonable to suppose that the fondest expressions of remembrance from a world, which he has served and enlightened, can be displeasing to the spirit of "a just man made perfect;" since we are taught by Religion, that the gratitude of mankind is acceptable even to GOD. I endeavoured to convince my companion, that, as the Publick had seen in HOWARD a person who reflected more genuine honour on our country than any of her Philosophers, her Poets, her Orators, her Heroes, or Divines, it is incumbent on the Nation to consult her own glory by commemorating, in the fullest manner, his beneficent exertions, and by establishing the dignity of his unrivaled virtue.

My arguments, and my zeal, made some impression on the mind of my antagonist; and sunk so deeply into my own, that on my retiring to rest they gave rise to the following vision.

I was suddenly transported to the confines of a region, which astonished me by its loveliness and extent; it was called, The Paradise of true Glory. As I approached the entrance, my eyes were delightfully fascinated by two beings of human form, who presided over the portal. Their names were Genius and Sensibility:—it was their office to gratify with a view of this Paradise every mortal that revered them sincerely; and to reject only such intruders as presumed to treat either the one or the other with the insolence of disdain, or the coldness of contempt: an incident that I should have thought impossible, from the transcendent beauty which is visible in each; but, to my surprize, they informed me it very frequently happened.

As I readily paid them the unsuspected homage of my soul, I was graciously permitted to pass the gate.—Immediately as I entered, I was saluted with a seraphic smile, by two benignant and inseparable Spirits: these were Gratitude and Admiration, the joint rulers of the dominion—"You are welcome," said the first, in a tone of angelic tenderness—"You are welcome to a scene utterly new to your senses, and in harmony with your heart: you delight in the praises of the deserving: and you are now wafted to a spot, where those who have merited highly of mankind are praised in proportion to their desert, and where the praise of exalted merit is fondly listened to by an extensive human audience, here purified by our supernatural agency from all the low and little jealousies of the earth."

I had hardly answered this pleasing information by a grateful obeisance to my radiant informer, when I perceived, in a gorgeous prospect that now opened before us, three structures of stupendous size and superior magnificence. The first was situated in a grove of olives, and appeared to me like an ancient temple of Attica, remarkable for massive strength, and a sober dignity—the second was less solid, but richer in decoration; and seemed to be almost surrounded by every tree and plant on which Nature has bestowed any salutary virtue: the third was shaded only by palms; the form of it was so wonderfully grand and aweful, that it struck me as a sanctuary for every pure and devout spirit from all the nations of the globe.

"These structures, that you survey with astonishment," said one of my benevolent conductors, "are devoted to what you mortals denominate the three liberal professions, Law, Medicine, and Theology. Whoever has a claim to distiguished honour from any one of the three, has a just encomium pronounced upon his services by the temporary President of that particular fabrick, in which he is entitled to such grateful remembrance." "Alas!" I replied, with a murmur that I could not suppress, "the Man whose well-deserved praises I most anxiously expected to hear in this region, belonged not to any one of these eminent classes in human life—he had no profession but that of Humanity."

"Be patient," said the sweetest of my aetherial guides, with a rebuke that was softened by a smile of indulgence! "Let not your zeal for the honour of an individual, however meritorious, make you unjust, or insensible, to the merit of others! Assume the temper of this region, where praise is distributed by equity and affection, but where prejudice and partiality are not allowed to intrude!—Let us advance," continued my monitor, with an encouraging movement of her hand; "it is time that I should lead you to the nearest assembly."

I obeyed with reverential silence; and as I passed the vestibule of the majestic edifice, my heart panted with an aweful expectation of beholding the shades of Solon, Lycurgus, and other departed Legislators, from the various nations of the world. I was chearfully surprized by a very different spectacle.

The capacious structure was filled with a concourse of living mortals, lively, yet respectable in their appearance, evidently belonging to many countries; but all, as I perceived by their habits, connected with the Law. Throughout all the multitude I heard no sound of dissention or debate: but over all there reigned an air of intelligence and sympathy, while all were hushed in silent expectance, and eager attention, with their eyes directed to an elevated tribunal:—On this a personage was sitting, whose majestic figure I immediately recollected. His countenance is marked with that austerity and grandeur, which are the external characteristicks of Law herself. His heart, as those who know it ultimately declare, expresses the tender and beneficent influence of that Power, who is the acknowledged parent of security and comfort. With a voice that pervaded the most distant recesses of the extensive dome, and in tones that sunk deep into the bosom of every auditor, he pronounced the following oration:

"After passing many years of life in the painful investigation of human offences, it is with peculiar satisfaction that I find myself commissioned to commemorate, in this Assembly, a character of virtue without example—a character, at once so meek and so sublime, that, if a feeling spirit had been poisoned with misanthropy from too close a contemplation of mortal crimes, this character alone might serve as an antidote to the word of mental distempers, and awaken the most callous and sarcastic mind to confess the dignity of our Nature, and the beneficence of our God. In stating to you the merits of HOWARD, I might expatiate with delight on the various qualities of this incomparable man; I might trace his progress through the different periods of a life always singular and always instructive. I could not be checked by any fear of overstepping the modesty of Truth in the celebration of Virtue, so solid and so extensive, that the malevolence of Envy could not diminish its weight, the fondness of Enthusiasm could not amplify its effects. But I must not forget that there are professional limits to my discourse. It is incumbent on me to confine myself to a single object, and to dwell only on those public services, that peculiarly endear the name of Howard to the liberal and enlightened community in which I have the honour to preside.

"It was in the capacity of a Minister to Justice, that the pure spirit, whom it is my glory to praise, first conceived the idea of those unrivaled labours that have rendered his memory a treasure to mankind. In discharging a temporary office, that exposed to him the condition of criminals, he was led to meditate on the evils which had grievously contaminated the operations of Justice. He perceived that Law herself, like one of her most illustrious Delegates (I mean the immortal Bacon), was grossly injured by the secret and sordid enormities of her menial servants: that Captivity and Coercion, those necessary supporters of her power, instead of producing good, often gave birth to mischiefs more flagrant, and more fatal, than those which they were employed to correct. He found, even in the prisons of his own humane and enlightened country, an accumulation of the most hideous abuses: he found them not nurseries of penitence and amendment, but schools of vice and impiety; or dens of filth, famine, and disease: not the seats of just and salutary correction and punishment, but the strong holds of cruelty and extortion. The irons of the prisoner, which he only beheld, entered into his soul, and awakened unextinguishable energy in a spirit, of which companion and fortitude were the divine characteristicks. In the noble emotions of pity for the oppressed, and of zeal for the honour and interest of civilized society, he conceived perhaps the sublimest design that ever occupied and exalted the mind of man, the design to search and to purify the polluted stream of Penal Justice, not only throughout his own country, but through the various nations of the world. How low, how little, are the grandest enterprizes of Heroic Ambition, when compared with this magnanimous pursuit! How frivolous and vain are the highest aims of Fancy and Science, when contrasted with a purpose so beneficently great! But, marvellous as the magnitude of HOWARD'S enterprise appears, on the slightest view that magnitude becomes doubly striking, when we contemplate at the same time the many circumstances that might either allure or deter him from the prosecution of his idea. Consider him as a private gentleman, possessed of ease and independence, accustomed to employ and amuse his mind in retired study and philosophical speculation; arrived at that period of life, when the springs of activity and enterprize in the human frame have begun to lose their force! consider that his health, even in youth, had appeared unequal to common fatigue! his stature low! his deportment humble! his voice almost effeminate! Such was the wonderful being, who relinquished the retirement, the tranquillity, the comforts, that he loved and enjoyed, to embark in labours at which the most hardy might tremble; to plunge in perils from which the most resolute might recede without a diminution of honour. Under all these apparent disadvantages, unsummoned, unauthorized by any Prince, unexcited by any popular invitation, he resolved to investigate all the abuses of imprisonment; to visit the abodes of wretchedness and infection; and to prove himself the friend of the friendless, in every country that the limits of his advanced life would allow him to examine. Against such an enterprize, projected by such an individual, what forcible arguments might be urged, not only by every selfish passion, but even by that prudence, and that reason, which are allowed to regulate an elevated mind! How plausibly did Friendship exclaim to Howard, 'Your projects are unquestionably noble; but they are above the execution of any individual: you are unarmed with authority; you have the wish to do great good, but the power of doing little! Consider the probable issue of the undertaking!—You will see a few hapless wretches, and tell their condition to the inattentive world; perhaps perish yourself from contagion, before you have time to tell it; and leave your afflicted friends to lament your untimely fate, and the ungrateful Publick to deride your temerity!' What force of intellect, what dignity of soul were required to prevent a mortal from yielding to remonstrances so engaging! The divine energy of Genius and of Virtue enabled HOWARD to foresee, that the sanctity of his pursuit would supply him with strength and powers far superior to all human authority:—His piercing mind comprehended that there are enormities of such a nature, that to survey and to reveal them is to effect their correction.—He felt that his sincere compassion for the oppressed, and his ardent desire to promote perfect justice, would serve him as a perpetual antidote against the poison of fear.—He felt that in the darkness of dungeons he should want no associates, no guards to defend him against the outrages of detected extortion, or suspicious brutality.—He felt, that as his purpose was heavenly, the powers of Heaven would be displayed in his support; that iniquity and oppression would not dare to lift a hand against him, though they knew it was the business of his life to annihilate their sway in their most secret dominion. How admirably did the progress of his travels evince and justify the pure and enlightened confidence of his spirit! All dangers, all difficulties, vanish before his gentleness, his regularity, his perseverance. Insolence and ferocity seem to turn, at his approach, into docility and respect. Every hardship he endures, every step he advances, in his wide and laborious career of Beneficence, instead of impairing his strength, invigorates his frame; instead of diminishing his influence, increases the utility of his conduct, by making the world acquainted with the sanctity of his character. Witness, ye various regions of the earth! with what surprize, delight, and veneration, ye beheld an unarmed, and unassuming traveller instructing you in the sublime science of mitigating human misery, and giving you a matchless example of tenderness and magnanimity! O, England! thou generous country! ever enamoured of glory, contemplate in this, the most perfect of thy illustrious sons; contemplate those virtues, and that honour, in which thy parental spirit may most happily exult!—What spectacle can be more flattering to thy native, thy honest pride, than to behold the proudest potentates of distant nations listening with pleasure to a private Englishman; and learning, from his researches, how to relieve the most injured of their subjects! how to abolish the enormities of perverted Justice! To form a complete account of the good arising to the world from the life and labours of Howard, would be a task beyond the limits of any human mind: an exact statement of the benefits he has conferred upon society, could be rendered only by the attendant Spirit whom Providence commissioned to watch over him, and who might discern, by the powers of supernatural vision, what pregnant sources of public calamity he crushed in the seed, and what future virtues, in various individuals, he may draw into the service of mankind by the attraction of his example.

"Of good, more immediately visible, which his exertions produced, there is abundant evidence in his own country. In the wide circle of his foreign excursion, what nation, what city, does not bear some conspicuous traces of his intrepid and indefatigable beneficence! Of the astonishing length to which his zeal and perseverance extended, we have the most ingenuous and satisfactory narration in those singularly meritorious volumes which he has given to the world. In these we behold the minute detail of labours to which there is nothing similar, or second, in the history of public virtue; and for which there could be no adequate reward but in the beatitude of Heaven. An eloquent Enthusiast, whose genius was nearly allied to frenzy, has expressed a desire to present himself before the tribunal of the Almighty Judge, with a volume in his hand, in which he had recorded his own thoughts and actions: if such an idea could be suitable to the littleness of man, if it could become any mortal of faculties so limited to make such an offering to the great Fountain of all intelligence, that mortal must assuredly be Howard: for where could we find another individual, not professedly inspired, who might present to his Maker a record of labours so eminently directed by Piety and Virtue! a book, addressed to mankind, without insulting their weakness, or flattering their passions! a book, whose great object was to benefit the world, without seeking from it any kind of reward! a book, in which the genuine modesty of the Writer is equal to his unexampled beneficence! The mind of

Howard was singularly and sublimely free from the common and dangerous passion for applause: that passion which, though taken altogether, it is certainly beneficial to the interests of mankind, yet frequently communicates inquietude and unsteadiness to the pursuits of Genius and Virtue. As human praise was never the object of his ambition, so he has nobly soared above it. There appear, in different ages upon the Earth, certain elevated spirits, who, by the sublimity of their conceptions, and the magnanimity of their conduct, attain a degree of glory which can never be reached by the keenest followers of Fame—They seek not panegyricks; and panegyricks can add nothing to their honour. The Eulogies have perished which were devoted by the luxuriant genius of Tully, and by the laconic spirit of Brutus, to the public virtue of Cato; yet the name of that illustrious Roman is still powerful in the world, and excites in every cultivated mind, an animating idea of independent integrity. The name of Howard has superior force, and a happier effect. It is a sound, at which the strings of humanity will vibrate with exultation in many millions of hearts. Through the various nations that he visited, the mere echo of his name will be sufficient to awaken that noblest sensibility, which at once softens and elevates the soul. Every warm hearted and worthy individual who mentions Howard will glow with an honest, a generous satisfaction, in feeling himself the fellow-creature of such a man. Wherever the elegant arts are established, they will contend in raising memorials to his honour. Indeed, the globe itself may be considered as his Mausoleum; and the inhabitants of every prison it contains, as groups of living statues that commemorate his virtue. There is no class of mankind by whom his memory ought not to be cherished, because all are interested in those evils (so pernicious to society! so dangerous to life!) which he was ever labouring to lessen or exterminate. It might be wished, that different communities should separately devise some different tribute of respect to him whose character and conduct is so interesting to all: not for the sake of multiplying vain and useless offerings to the dead, but to impress with more energy and extent his ennobling remembrance on the heart and soul of the living. It is hardly possible to present too frequently to the human mind the image of a man who lived only to do good. I mean not merely such a resemblance of his form as Art may execute with materials almost as perishable as the image of human clay, but such an impression of his soul as may have a more lasting influence on the life and conduct of his admirers, such as, diffusing among them a portion of his spirit, may in some measure perpetuate his existence.

"By this community, I am confident, such public honours will be paid to HOWARD, as may be most suitable to the peculiar interest which it becomes us to take in his glory. What these honours shall be is a point to be settled by this liberal and enlightened Assembly, which assuredly will not fail to remember that he suggested to Legal Authority her omissions and defects with the modest and endearing tenderness of a Friend; that he laboured in the service of Justice with that intelligence, fortitude, and zeal, which her votaries cannot too warmly admire, or too gratefully acknowledge."

The President arose as he thus ended his speech; and the members of the Assembly seemed beginning to confer among themselves; but what debates ensued, or what measure was adopted, I am unable to tell, as my visionary Guides immediately hurried me to the adjoining Temple.

This second structure, though less extensive and less solid than the first, was more attractive to the eye, as it abounded with scientifical and diversified decorations. The Assembly consisted of men, who appeared to me equally remarkable for keenness of intellect and elegance of manners. The seat of pre eminence among them was filled by a person who possessed in a very uncommon degree these two valuable qualities, so happily conducive to medical utility and medical distinction. Though left a young orphan, without patrimony, and obliged to struggle with early disadvantages, he raised himself by meritorious exertion to the head of a profession in which opulence is generally the just attendant on knowledge and reputation. But neither opulence, nor his long intercourse with sickness and death, have hardened the native tenderness of his heart; and I had lately known him shed tears of regret on the untimely fate of an amiable patient, whom his consummate skill and attention were unable to save.

Thus strongly prepossessed in his favour, I was delighted to observe that he was preparing to address the Assembly in the moment we entered. My celestial Guides smiled on each other in perceiving my satisfaction; and being placed by them instantaneously in a commodious situation, I heard the following discourse; which the character I have described delivered with an ease and refined acuteness peculiar to himself, never raising his voice above the pitch of polite and spirited conversation:

"I am persuaded, that every individual to whom I have now the happiness of speaking, will readily agree with me in this sentiment, that we cannot possibly do ourselves more honour as a Fraternity than by considering HOWARD as an Associate: assuredly, there is no class of men who may more justly presume to cherish his name and character with a fraternal affection. In proportion as we are accustomed to contemplate, to pity, and to counteract, the sufferings of Nature, the more are we enabled and inclined to estimate, to love, and to revere, a being so compassionate and beneficent. If Physicians are, what I once heard them called by a lively friend, the Soldiers of Humanity, engaged in a perpetual, and too often, alas! unsuccessful conflict against the enemies of life; HOWARD is not only entitled to high rank in our corps, but he is the very Caesar of this hard, this perilous, and, let me add, this most honourable warfare. Perhaps the ambition of the great Roman Commander, insatiate and sanguinary as it was, did not contribute more to the torment and destruction of the human race, than the charity of the English Philanthropist has contributed to its relief and preservation. Of this we are very certain, the splendid and indefatigable Hero of Slaughter and Vain-glory did not traverse a more extensive field, nor expose himself more courageously to personal danger, than our meek and unostentatious Hero of Medical Benevolence. In point of true magnanimity, I apprehend the spirit of Caesar would very willingly confess, that his own celebrated attempts to reduce Gaul and Britain were low and little achievements, when compared to the unexampled efforts by which Howard endeavoured to exterminate or subdue (those enemies more terrific) the Gaol Fever, and the Plague.

"But leaving it to more able and eloquent panegyrists to celebrate the originality, the boldness, and all the various merit of his philanthropic exertions, I shall confine myself to a few remarks, and chiefly professional ones, on his invaluable character. It appears to me highly worthy of observation, that Howard, before he entered on his grand projects of Public Benevolence, was subject to those little, but depressive variations of health which have betrayed many a valetudinarian into habits of inaction and inutility. Happily for himself, and for mankind, this excellent person surmounted a constitutional bias to indolence and retirement. The consequence sequence was, he became a singular example of activity and vigour. His powers, and enjoyments of bodily and mental health, augmented in proportion to the extensive utility of his pursuits.

"Beneficial as his life has been to the world, his memory may be still more so. It may prove a perpetual blessing to mankind, if it dissipates, as it ought to do, a weak and common prejudice, which often operates as a palsy upon the first idea of a great and generous undertaking. The prejudice I mean is a hasty persuasion, frequently found in the most amiable minds, that some peculiar strength of nerve, some rare mechanism of frame, and extraordinary assemblage of mental powers, are absolutely requisite for the execution of any noble design. How greatly does it redound to the true glory of Howard to have given in his successful labours the fullest refutation of a prejudice, so inimical to the interest and the honour of human-nature! a prejudice, by whose influence, to use the words of our great Poet,

-The native hue of Resolution
sicklied o'er with the pale cast of Fear,
d enterprizes of great pith and moment,
th this regard, their currents turn awry
d lose the name of action."

"The life and character of Howard, if they are justly considered, may not only annihilate this pernicious prejudice, but tend to establish an opposite and consolatory truth. His example may shew us, that some degrees of bodily weakness and mental depression may be most happily cured by active exertion in the service of mankind. Perhaps there never existed a more striking proof how far a noble impulse, communicated to the mind by a project of extensive Benevolence, may invigorate a frame not equal in health, strength, and stature, to the common standard of men. It is a prudential maxim of the celebrated Raleigh, that 'Whosoever will live altogether out of himself, and study other men's humours, shall never be unfortunate;' a maxim, which the example of Howard might almost teach us to convert into a medical aphorism by saying, 'Whosoever will live altogether out of himself, and consult other men's wants, and calamities, shall never be unhealthy.' It is delightful to those, who detest the debasing tenets of a selfish philosophy, to see the happy influence of opposite ideas; to observe (what Physicians have frequent opportunities of observing), that as a selfish turn of mind often attracts and encreases the malignity of sickness, so an unselfish, a compassionate spirit has a natural tendency to escape or subdue it. What can be more pleasing to those, who assert and esteem the dignity of human-nature, than to see, that the having lost all thoughts of self, and having acted in direct opposition to selfish principles, has promoted even the personal advantage of a generous individual? From such a series of philanthropic labour and peril, as a selfish and timid mind might esteem it frenzy to encounter, Howard derived not only his unrivalled and immortal reputation, but the perfect restoration of enfeebled health; not to mention those high gratifications of the heart and conscience, which are superior to all the enjoyments both of health and glory. With such temperance in diet, that his daily food would appear to most people not sufficient to support the common functions of life, he chearfully sustained the hardships of long travel, through regions where travelling is most difficult and dangerous. With a figure, voice, and deportment, that seemed to preclude him from all personal influence and authority; and with no mental acquisitions, except those which are common to every cultivated mind, he secured to himself not only universal admiration, but, I may venture to say, the just and moral idolatry of the world. So invigorating are projects of extensive Beneficence! so powerful is the energy of Public Virtue!

"Never, indeed, was the astonishing influence of plain and simple goodness more strikingly displayed, than in the deference and respect which this private and meek individual received, not only from foreign and imperious Rulers of the Earth, but from hardened and atrocious wretches, on whom Justice herself could hardly make any mental impression, though armed with all the splendour, and all the violence of power. Two particular examples of the influence I am speaking of, I shall mention here, not only as honourable to the prime object of our regard, but as they may suggest to contemplative minds some useful ideas, by shewing how far the mere weight of an upright and benevolent character alone may give to the most callous nerves a trembling sensibility, and awaken the most ferocious spirit to self-correction.

"When our indefatigable Visitor of prisons was in Russia, he beheld, in public, the punishment of the knoot severely administered by a strong and stern executioner.

"On the following day he waited on this man, to request from him various information. The executioner attended him obsequiously; but this athletic savage, though trained to acts of cruelty, and conscious he had a legal sanction for the barbarous violence he had exerted, could not behold without shuddering the meek and gentle Missionary of Compassion.

"The second and more memorable example of his singular influence occurred in a prison of his own country, and relates to an outrageous female delinquent. A corrupt and ferocious woman is, perhaps, the most intractable fiend that human benevolence can attempt to reform; but even this difficulty the mild and and powerful character of HOWARD accomplished.

"In one of our Western gaols, he found an unhappy female loaded with heavy irons: on his appearance she entreated him to obtain for her the removal of these galling fetters. Upon enquiry, he found that many endeavours had been made to keep this turbulent offender in proper subjection without the severity of chains; but, after repeated promises of amendment on milder treatment, she had obliged the keeper to have recourse to this extreme by relapsing into the most flagrant and insufferable contempt of decency and order. Upon this information, HOWARD said mildly to the unhappy criminal, 'I wish to relieve you, but you put it out of my power; for I should lose all the little credit I have, if I exerted it for offenders so hardened and so turbulent.' 'I know,' replied the intractable delinquent, 'I know that I have a proud and rebellious spirit; but if I give a promise to so good a man as you are, I can and I will command it.' On this firm assurance of reformation, the benevolent HOWARD became a kind of surety for her future peaceable conduct on the removal of her irons; and he had the inexpressible delight to find, on his next visit to the prisoners of this gaol, that the outrageous and ungovernable culprit, for whom he had ventured to answer, was become the most orderly among them.

"I could wish, for the moral interest of mankind, that it were possible to obtain a minute account of the services rendered to the calamitous spirit of many a forsaken individual by the singular charity of HOWARD. What could be more instructive than to observe how his Beneficence encreased by its exertion and success; while his desire of befriending the wretched became, as it were, the vital spirit that gave strength and duration to his own existence!

"If we contemplate with pleasure the singular re-establishment of bodily health, which HOWARD derived from his active philanthropy; it may be still more pleasing to recollect, that it also afforded him an efficacious medicine for an afflicted mind. Perhaps it was to shew the full efficacy of this virtue in all its lustre, that Heaven allotted to this excellent personage a domestic calamity, which appears (to borrow an expression from a great writer) 'of an unconscionable size to human strength.'

"That capricious and detestable spirit of Detraction, which on Earth never fails to persecute superior Virtue, has not scrupled to assert that the affliction, to which I allude, was the mere consequence of paternal austerity. The Earth itself, though frequently accused of being eager to receive ideas that may abase the eminent, could hardly admit a calumny so groundless and irrational. In this purer spot it is utterly needless to prove the innocence of an exalted being, to whom we are only solicitous to pay that sincere tribute of praise and veneration which we are conscious he deserves. In truth, this admirable Character seemed to illustrate the philosophical maxim, that mildness is the proper companion of true magnanimity. He had a gentleness of manners, that was peculiar to himself; and, instead of possessing such imperious severity of spirit as might produce the calamity I allude to, he was really endued with such native tenderness of heart as must have sunk under it, had he not found in the unexampled services that he rendered to the world, an antidote to the poison of domestic infelicity. It is among the most gracious ordinances of Providence, that man is sure to find the most powerful relief for his own particular afflictions, in his endeavours to alleviate the sufferings of others. And permit me to add, it is this beneficent law of our nature, that gives a peculiar charm and dignity to the Medical Profession; a profession singularly endeared to the affectionate HOWARD! not only as its compassionate and active spirit was the guide of his pursuits, but as one of its prime ornaments was his favourite associate and his bosom-friend. If different classes of men are to vie with each other, as it may certainly become them to do, in rendering various honours to this their matchless Benefactor; I hope we shall display, with the most affectionate spirit, the deep interest that we ought to take in his glory. I think it very desirable that every Physician should possess a Medal of HOWARD, not only to shew his veneration for the great Philanthropist, but to derive personal advantage from such a mental Amulet, if I may hazard the expression. Most of us, in the exercise of Medicine, feel at particular moments that our spirits are too sensibly affected by the objects we survey; that scenes of misery and infection depress and alarm: at such a time how might it rekindle the energy of our minds to contemplate a little effigy of HOWARD! to recollect, that all the trouble and danger that we encounter, in the practice of a lucrative profession, are trifling in the extreme, when compared to the labour and the peril, which this wonderful man most willingly took upon himself, without looking forward to any reward but the approbation of Heaven!

"I mention not a Medal as a new idea—it has been already in contemplation; and a motto for it suggested, which applies with such singular force and propriety to the person whom it is designed to commemorate, that perhaps the wide range of classical literature could not afford another passage so strikingly apposite to a character so extraordinary—

upuere patres tentamina tanta,

natusque tuos: pro te Reus ipse timebat."—

"I must confess, however, that I wish for another, which may seem to bind him more closely to us in a medical point of view. But it is time to leave the different members of our Fraternity at full liberty to propose any marks of distinction that they wish to suggest.—It is sufficient for me to have reminded you of a truth, which I am confident we all equally feel, that, while we justly consider ourselves as students in the extensive school of Humanity, it becomes us to look up to HOWARD, with a laudable veneration, as the Prince and Patron of our Order."

On the conclusion of this discourse, my Guides immediately conducted me, with their former celerity and kindness, to the only remaining Structure. It was the most extensive, and, from the hallowed majesty of its appearance, the most admirable of the three. In approaching it, I paused a moment in aweful surprise at the solemnity of the fabrick: the most lovely and communicative of my two aetherial conductors smiled upon me, and said, "You will find here Ministers of GOD from every Christian country; but only those who consider Evangelical Charity as the essence of true Religion, and who are disposed to honour, in the favourite object of your veneration, the most signal example of that virtue, which the present age has beheld." "I hope then," I eagerly replied, "I shall have the delight of hearing, on this occasion, the most eloquent of our English Bishops." On this exclamation, my kind informer regarded me with that lively and soothing air with which intelligent Benevolence corrects mistaken simplicity, and thus continued to instruct me with united vivacity and tenderness.

"Earthly distinctions, you know, are of little moment in the sight of Heaven. You will hear no Prelate; and perhaps you may feel surprised and indignant, when you observe how very few of your Mitred Countrymen are to be seen in this Assembly; but you will not retain in this hallowed spot that most common of human infirmities, a tendency to censure or to suspicion. You will recollect that this Convocation contains only those charitable men, who are peculiarly disposed to honour your recent model of this Christian virtue. Other good men may exist, who, from motives of innocent mistake, or of mere inadvertency, may fail to exhibit that animated regard to his exemplary character, which assuredly it has merited from all men, and which the Ministers of Religion may most properly display.

"One of these," continued my Director, "you are now going to hear; not, indeed, a Dignitary of your Church, yet a Divine of Talents, Learning, and Charity. He was led, by a laudable warmth of heart, to suggest to your Country the first idea of paying a public tribute of veneration to the signal virtue of Howard; and has acquired from this circumstance a title to commemorate here the merit, to which he was eager to render such early justice on earth. But it is time for us to attend him."

We immediately entered the temple; and I beheld an Ecclesiastic rising at that moment to address a very numerous Assembly of his order, that seemed to contain Christians of every sect, and Ministers of every degree. The person preparing to speak was distinguished by a majestic comeliness of person, though he appeared to have passed the middle age of life; and with a powerful elocution he delivered the following discourse.

"The Righteous are bold as a Lion."

Proverbs, chap, xxviii, ver. i.

"In these few words, my brethren, we have a passage of Scripture, that served as a favourite maxim, or leading truth, to the admirable personage whose glorious qualities it is now both my duty and my delight to recall to your remembrance. The words, indeed, are so consonant to that exalted spirit which his life displayed, that they almost appear to me an epitome of his character. Let us consider Courage as one of his principal endowments! To contemplate so pure and resolute a being in this point of view, may lead us to form just ideas on the true nature of this primary virtue, on the sacred source from whence it should proceed, and the sublime end to which it should aspire. How large a portion of folly, vice, and wickedness, have arisen from mere mistakes concerning this most important of human qualities! so important, that the real dignity of man can only rise in proportion as this virtue is perfectly understood, and properly cherished! In the same proportion, let me add, our courageous Philanthropist will be found entitled to the praise of every upright mind, to the homage of every feeling heart.

"If we take the word Courage" in the most common and simple sense of that term, as a generous and noble contempt of personal hardship and danger; who has given more numerous or more striking examples of such brave contempt! Or if we follow the definition of Courage given us by a profound, an eloquent, and philanthropic Writer, namely, that it is a just estimate of our own powers; who is there among the most signal Benefactors of mankind, not professedly inspired, that ever formed an estimate of what he might achieve in the most glorious field of enterprize, at once so difficult, and so true, so humble, and so grand.

"With every apparent disadvantage, Howard conceived it possible that his endeavours might correct the abuses, and mitigate the sufferings of men, in various nations of the world. Whence happened it, that a mortal, so visibly weak and gentle, shrunk not from an idea so pregnant with difficulty and peril! It was because, 'The Righteous are bold as a Lion.' It was because he felt the strongest internal conviction of this animating truth, that, while Heaven blesses a man with health sufficient to pursue a benevolent and magnanimous design, the vigour of his mind, and most probably his powers of doing good, will be proportioned to the firmness of his faith, and the sincerity of his virtue.

"Many achievements of beneficent Courage have undoubtedly been accomplished by men influenced by no motive but that generous love of glory which is so frequently the predominant passion of an active and ardent mind: but the virtues that arise from this source are as unsteady, and as precarious, as the reward they pursue. He who acts only as a candidate for the applause of mankind, will find his spirit vary with all the variations in the ever-changing atmosphere of popular opinion. He will be subject to hot and cold fits of action and inactivity, of confidence and distrust, in proportion as the illusive vapour, that he follows, may either sparkle or fade before him. Hence proceeded much of that inconsistency and weakness, which appear in some of the most enlightened, and exalted characters of the Pagan world.—Wanting a purer light from Heaven, the most radiant spirits of antiquity were bewildered; one in particular, the mildest and most undaunted of antient Worthies, who had a sufficient portion of heroic philanthropy to prefer the benefit of mankind to every selfish consideration, had yet his hours of diffidence and despondency. On a final review of his own generous labours, he is supposed to have questioned the very existence of Virtue, though he had made it the idol of his life; a striking proof, that the temperate and invariable energy of soul, which alone perhaps deserves the name of true Courage, can only proceed from a fuller knowledge and love of GOD; from the animating assurance, that, however we may prosper or fail in the earthly success of our endeavours to do good, the merit of the attempt is registered in Heaven; and we secure to ourselves the everlasting approbation of our Almighty Parent, in proportion as we approach towards that blessed model of Perfect Benevolence, who has taught us, by his divine example, to compassionate and to relieve the sufferings of the wretched. From this source flowed the courageous beneficence of HOWARD: and how delightful it is to observe that the force, the extent, the utility, and the lustre of the stream, has gloriously corresponded to the height and purity of the fountain!

"The Sensualist and the Sceptic may, indeed, deride the conduct of a man, who sacrificed all the common pleasures of life, and sought for no recompence but in the favour of Heaven. It may be said that an illusive fervor of mind has hurried men, in all periods of the world, into singular and wild exertions, which excite the wonder of the passing hour, and are afterwards either deservedly forgotten, or only recalled to notice by Reason and Philosophy, to caution the restless and impetuous spirit of man against all similar excesses.

"But the pursuits of Howard, though they had all that sublime energy which so often distinguished the projects of Superstition, were so far from being influenced by any superstitious propensity, that perhaps they cannot appear to more advantage than by being brought into comparison, or contrast, not with the sluggish piety of sequestered Monks, but with the bold and splendid feats of the most active and enterprising Fanaticism. Allow me, therefore, to recall to your thoughts those distant ages, when every ardent spirit in Christendom was inflamed with a passionate desire to deliver the Christian pilgrims of Palestine from the oppression of Infidels! Figure to yourselves the whole force of Europe collecting its violence, like a troubled sea, and preparing to pour a terrific and destructive inundation over the Holy Land! Behold the strong and the weak, the ambitious and the humble, pursuing the same object! Behold assembled Kings and their People, Soldiers and Priests, the servants of Earth and Heaven rushing, with equal ardour, to rescue the Sepulchre of Christ, and to drown all the innumerable enemies of their Faith in an universal deluge of blood! In this scene we have the sublimest spectacle, perhaps, that was ever exhibited by mistaken piety and misguided valour. The love of God, by which this heroic multitude was professedly impelled, was probably in many minds as sincere as it was ardent. The religious spirit of their enterprize can still animate and transport us in the song of the Poet: and in the more rational page of History, while we justly lament the errors of their devotion, we admire the force and perseverance of their courage.

"To the sublime fortitude of these collected warriors, let us compare the mild magnanimity of HOWARD. Let us survey him setting forth for an expedition as perilous as theirs; not as the Soldier of Fanaticism, but as the Pilgrim of Humanity! Attachment to GOD, and resolution which no hardship, no danger, no difficulty can daunt, are equally conspicuous in the sanguinary Fanatic and the compassionate Philanthropist: but how widely different are the prime earthly objects of their pursuits! The fierce Crusaders invaded Asia with a desire to exterminate the Infidels. The benevolent HOWARD was led into the same quarter of the globe, and into perils more deadly than those of war, by a wish to exterminate, or rather to restrain, the ravages of that terrific enemy to human life, the Plague.

"He had conceived an idea, that, as this most alarming of mortal maladies has been often strangely neglected by the sluggish and superstitious inhabitants of the East, it might be possible by a calm and courageous examination of its nature and its progress, to set limits to its rage; and particularly to secure his own country from a future visitation of a calamity, against which the fearless and eager spirit of Commerce appears not to have established a sufficient precaution. For the prospect of accomplishing public good, so devoutly to be wished, he nobly thought it a trifling sacrifice to hazard the little remnant of his advanced life; and, however men or nations may differ in policy or religion, whereever there is a human spirit sufficiently pure and enlightened to estimate public virtue, the sentiments and the conduct of HOWARD must secure to his memory the fondest veneration. There is a perfection and felicity in his character that appears supremely laudable in every point of view. If, abstracted from all religious considerations, we regard him only as a citizen who devoted himself to the service of his country, the brightest records of Antiquity afford us no parallel to his merit. Had he lived in those early times, the generous enthusiasm of the antient world would have idolized his name. Philosophy and Genius would have found, in his benevolent labours, the most ample theme for instruction, and the purest subject for universal panegyrick. They would have celebrated him as a benefactor to mankind, who had built a new portico to the Temple of Glory superior to the dome itself. They would have preferred the beneficent Philanthropist to the dazzling Conqueror, to the fascinating Demagogue, to the attractive Sophist; and all the various idols of public praise. But as Antiquity exhibits no character of such unclouded lustre, we have great reason to conclude, that such a character could owe its existence only to the pure and sublime spirit of our Christian Faith. Let us, therefore, contemplate HOWARD as a Christian! it is by considering him in this light, that we shall feel ourselves most happily related to his virtues, and most delightfully interested in the honours they receive.

"In the poor and calamitous objects of his regard, in the gentleness and purity of his manners, in his modest and magnanimous refusal of earthly honours, in the wide extent and courageous perseverance of his charity, we cannot fail to discern how richly he was endowed with the genuine spirit of that pure and sublime Religion which has the divine prerogative of converting weakness into strength, and of giving to Humility the influence of Power. There is not a feature in the character, there is hardly an action in the life of this exemplary personage, that does not mark him as a true servant of CHRIST. And may we not presume the blessed Author of our faith, in supplying us in these dissolute times with a recent example of such astonishing and unlimited beneficence, is graciously pleased to afford us a new motive to prize and to cherish that animating faith, which could form, in an age like the present, a character so wonderfully entitled to the veneration of the world? The spirit of Christianity is so visible in the conduct of HOWARD, that the prime objects of his attention might be thought to have been suggested to him by the very words in which our blessed Lord announces to the heirs of eternal glory the source of their beatitude—'Come, ye blessed of my Father, inherit the kingdom prepared for you from the foundation of the world; for I was an hungry, and ye gave me meat; I was thirsty, and ye gave me drink; I was a stranger, and ye took me in; naked, and ye cloathed me; I was sick, and ye visited me; I was in prison, and ye came unto me.'

"Is it possible for us, my Brethren, to recall to our memory these holy words without feeling at the same time, in the most forcible degree, all the Christian merits of HOWARD? Can we fail to admire and to venerate the unexampled ardour, purity, and perseverance, with which he exercised the peculiar virtue so distinguished by our Lord?—While we behold him sublimely pre-eminent in this Christian perfection, shall we not cherish the delightful idea, that his heavenly rewards will be finally adequate to his unrivaled labours on earth? Shall not those who have loved him exult in the persuasion, that in that great and aweful day, when the living and the dead are to receive their everlasting doom; when the princes and the great ones of the earth may be confronted with those whom they have persecuted and oppressed, or whom they have failed to relieve; when the proudest Sons of Learning, Genius, or Wit, may shrink at the superior lustre of those whom they have ridiculed and reviled; HOWARD will shine encircled by thousands, who will gratefully plead for his beatitude in those blessed words of our Redeemer, 'I was in prison, and he came unto me!'

"Yes, my Brethren, the day will assuredly come, when the servant so signally faithful will be called to a reward, surpassing the utmost reach of our conception, by the voice of his Righteous Master—then, and then only, will praise be fully proportioned to his transcendant merit; when this consummate Christian is raised to glory by the glorified Messiah, when his pure spirit exults in the commendation of his GOD.

"The imperfect efforts, that mankind may make to do honour to such a Being, cannot, indeed, so much promote his glory, as they may conduce to the interest of human nature. Subject as it has been to the wildest excesses, human panegyric, in all its shapes, may be safely devoted to a personage, whom it is hardly possible to praise with sincerity, without feeling our disposition improved. In a beneficent, a sublime, and truly religious character, there is a sort of magnetic virtue, which to those who are affectionately drawn towards it, though only in idea, communicates a portion of itself. Hence arises, what we cannot too fondly cherish, the delight and the utility of commemorating departed worth. If its title to commemoration be justly proportioned to its magnitude, its singularity, and extent; not only various individuals, but different Nations, will become rivals in promoting the fame of HOWARD. As the glorious qualities, which his life displayed, are equally open to the emulation of the great and the humble; every class of human creatures is peculiarly interested in his praise. If to honour his memory may be thought to belong to any one community more than to another; surely, my Brethren, we shall not fail to assume to ourselves so pleasing a duty, so honourable a distinction. Well, indeed, might the insulting enemies of our Faith reproach us with a supine and disgraceful inattention to the real interest of Virtue, and the true glory of Religion, could we suffer any other order of men to surpass the Ministers of CHRIST in a meritorious zeal to honour this faithful servant of Heaven, whose life exhibits a lesson more instructive and sublime than all the eloquence of the Pulpit! a Christian, who has shewn us, in the most signal manner, how practicable it is to follow, in succouring the distrest, not only the precepts, but the example of our GOD."

In the moment that this benevolent Divine concluded his address to his attentive brethren, my kind and vigilant Guides removed me from the temple.—I was now led into a scene entirely different from those we left. It was an open and verdant plain, with a few elevations in the ground, that afforded advantageous views of the whole extensive spot. Here, instead of beholding the Ministers of Peace, I found myself encircled by the multitudinous votaries of War. It appeared to me that all the military and all the naval servants of our country were collected together, and each different division of these well-appointed and well-looking men, that formed a pleasing spectacle alone, was attended by a crowd of miscellaneous spectators, more numerous than itself: yet in all this immense multitude there was no sign of tumult or confusion. They were ranged in such a manner as to form a wide circular area in the midst of them. I was stationed on a little eminence within this area; and in the same vacant space I beheld a party of veteran Commanders, both Military and Naval, who seemed to have been conferring together, but separated by the direction of my aetherial Conductors, to address, in different parts of this extensive field, the different companies assigned to their care. What they respectively said in their separate departments I was unable to discover, as I only heard distinctly one gallant Veteran, whose character was particularly dear to me. This consummate officer has raised himself by merit alone from the humblest rank of military life to a station of the highest honour and trust. His modesty is as singular as his fortune: passing close to me, with a gracious salutation, he approached a very fine orderly corps of foot, who looked up to him with a sort of filial respect, while he spoke to them the few following words:

"As bravery and compassion are the characteristics of good Soldiers, you cannot want, my friends, any long exhortation from me to honour the memory of HOWARD; the most resolute and the most compassionate man that has lived in our time. Though he was not of our profession, as his life was devoted to mitigate the united horrors of captivity and sickness, those worst of enemies to the spirit of a soldier, you will undoubtedly feel that he has a peculiar claim to our most grateful and generous regard."

This speech was followed by a burst of acclamation from those to whom it was particularly addressed. Similar shouts of applause resounded from different quarters of the spacious field, while our aetherial attendants, Gratitude and Admiration, who followed each speaker at the close of each address to different divisions of this innumerable assembly, displayed, to each division in its turn, an extensive sketch of a simple but magnificent mausoleum to the memory of Howard, in the form of an English lazaretto. On the first display of this striking and worthy monument, the applauding multitude seemed to exult in the prospect of its completion. But I soon observed, to my inexpressible concern, that while Gratitude and Admiration were busy in exciting the various ranks of the vast assembly, to accomplish this favourite design, they were followed by two earthy fiends of a dark and malignant influence: these were Detraction and Indifference, who shed such a chill and depressive mist around them, that all the ardour of the Assembly seemed to sink. Among the miscellaneous crowds that were visible between the divisions of the martial host, there ran a murmur of obloquy and derision against the pure object of public veneration. He was reviled as a whimsical Reformer, and a rash Enthusiast, who had absurdly sacrificed his life in a vain and fantastic pursuit. This base spirit of calumnious malignity was not communicated to any one division of the martial multitude; but the universal zeal for the glory of HOWARD seemed to be almost annihilated; even Gratitude and Admiration appeared to grow faint in their darling purpose. During their languor, they suffered their sketch of the Mausoleum to be gradually stolen from their hands, and to drop upon the ground. At this moment a sudden and violent earthquake was felt through all the extensive scene. The centre of the vacant area opened—it threw forth a phantom terrific and enormous—its magnitude seemed to grow upon the sight; its lineaments were shrouded from our view by an immense mantle, on which were represented a thousand different and hideous images of Death. Its name was Contagion—it rushed forward with an indescribable movement. Dismay and confusion overwhelmed all that quarter of the crowded scene, that was particularly threatened by its first advance. The affrighted multitude rolled back like a tumultuous sea. The horrid spectre stopt; and left a wide interval between itself and the retiring host. A ray of heavenly light illumined the vacant space. I fixed my eye on the brilliant spot, and soon beheld the meek and gentle form of HOWARD advancing, without fear or arrogance, towards the terrific Phantom. With an untrembling hand he seized the dark folds of its extensive mantle, and seemed animated with the hope of annihilating the Monster. In the instant, a burst of celestial splendor was spread over the gloomy plain. The Angel of Retribution descended; and snatching the consummate Philanthropist to his bosom, he rose again; while all the astonished multitude, now reviving from their terror, gazed only on the celestial apparition; and heard the reascending Seraph thus address the beneficent spirit now committed to his care:

"Thou faithful servant of Heaven! thy hour of recompence is come. Justly hast thou cautioned mankind not to impute thy conduct to rashness or enthusiasm. Weak and wavering in their own pursuits of felicity, thou wilt not wonder to see them so in their sense of thy merit, and their zeal for thy honour: but I am commissioned to bear thee to that All-seeing Power, who can alone truly estimate, and perfectly reward thy desert. I know that the praise of beings, inferior to thy GOD, never influenced thy life; but the homage of good minds is grateful to the purest inhabitants of Heaven; and in departing from a world so much indebted to thy virtue, let it gratify thy perfect spirit to foresee, that as long as the earth endures, the most enlightened of her sons will remember and revere thee as one of her sublimest benefactors."

As soon as the divine messenger had ceased to speak, every voice in the reanimated multitude, that heard him, raised a shout of benediction on the name of HOWARD. I started in transport at the sound; and the effort that I made to join the universal acclamation terminated my vision.

Pardon me, thou gentlest and most indulgent of Friends! that, conscious as I am of the sincerity with which thy pure mind ever wished to avoid all exuberance of praise, I yet presume to send into the world such a tribute to thy virtues as thy humility might reject. Let the motives of the publication atone for all its defects!

This little work is made public, not from a vain expectation, or desire, in the Writer to obtain any degree of literary distinction; for, if his wishes and endeavours are successful, the world will not know from what hand it proceeds.

Thou most revered object of my regard, who art looking down, perhaps, with compassion on the petty labours of various mortals, now trying to commemorate thy merit, thou seest that I am influenced by no arrogant conceit of having praised with peculiar felicity the perfections that I so ardently admire. No! I am perfectly sensible, that the most worthy memorial of thy virtues will be found in those pure records of thy public services which thy own hand has given to the world with all the amiable and affecting simplicity that distinguished thy character, and in the more comprehensive composition of some accomplished Biographer, who may have opportunities and ability to do justice to thy life.

The chief aim of these few and hasty pages is to recall, at this particular time, to the liberal spirits of our countrymen that generous ardour with which they embraced the first idea of a public monument to HOWARD. While the expence and dignity of that monument are yet unsettled, a Writer may consider himself as a friend to national honour, who endeavours to animate his country to the most extensive display of her munificence, and her gratitude towards the purest public virtue. May she justly remember, that, to testify a fond maternal pride in such a departed son, to manifest and perpetuate esteem for such a character, is, in truth, to promote the interest of genuine Patriotism, of sublime Morality, and of perfect Religion!

FINIS.

CPSIA information can be obtained
at www.ICGtesting.com
Printed in the USA
LVHW011240061021
699678LV00001B/84

9 789355 114105